PRIMARY SOURCES TEACHING KIT

The Civil War

Four score and seven years ago our fathers brought forth on this continent, a new nation, conceived in Liberty, and dedicated to the proposition that all men are created equal.

Now we are engaged in a great civil war, testing whether that nation, or any nation so conceived and so dedicated, can long endure. We are met on a great battlefield of that war. We have come to dedicate a portion of that field, as a final resting

by Karen Baicker

SCHOLASTIC
PROFESSIONALBOOKS

New York • Toronto • London • Auckland • Sydney
Mexico City • New Delhi • Hong Kong • Buenos Aires

for Paul Schmitz and Kim Groome

COVER DOCUMENTS: **Library of Congress:** Band of the 107th Colored Infantry [LC-B8171-7861]; Lincoln portrait; *Charleston Mercury* broadside; **The Museum of the Confederacy:** Union and Confederate Flags

INTERIOR DOCUMENTS: **Atlanta History Center,** Atlanta, GA: 27; **Bettmann/Corbis:** 34 (bottom); **Chicago Historical Society,** Chicago, IL: 19 (top right) [G1920.1274]; 19 (top left) [G1920.991]; 20 [IcHi-22030]; 37 [ICHi-22119]; **Comer Family Papers, Southern Historical Collection, The University of North Carolina at Chapel Hill,** NC: 26 (bottom) [#P-167]; **Corbis:** 1; 30; 31; 32 (top right and left); 33; 38; **Friends of the Hunley, Inc.,** Charleston, SC: 28 (bottom); **Library of Congress:** 23; 21 (center); 24 (bottom) [LC-USZ62-091075]; 25 (top) [LC-USZ62-312742]; 25 (bottom) [LC-USZ62-120309]; 26; 29 [LC-USZ62-091360]; 32 (bottom) [LC-B8171-7861]; 36 (right) [LC-MSS-44297-33-137]; 36 (left) [LC-MSS-44297-33-132]; 38 (top) [Rare books and manuscripts]; 40; 41; 42; **Museum of the Confederacy,** Richmond, VA: 28 (top); **National Archives:** 21 (top); **Rare Book Manuscript and Special Collections Library, Duke University,** Durham, NC: 22, 23; **Schomburg Center for Research in Black Culture, NYPL/American Tract Society:** 39; **South Carolina Historical Society** 19 (bottom left and right); **US Army Military History Institute:** 24 (top); **Wilson Library, University of North Carolina at Chapel Hill,** NC: 26 (bottom); 34 (top); 35

Edited by Sean Price
Picture research by Dwayne Howard
Cover design by Norma Ortiz
Interior design and illustration by Melinda Belter
ISBN: 0-590-37863-5

5 6 7 8 9 10   40   09 08 07 06 05

Contents

INTRODUCTION

Using Primary Sources in the Classroom

The Civil War may sound to your students like ancient history. And in fact, it is hard to believe that a war that ripped our country apart over such unfathomable issues took place relatively recently: less than 150 years ago. The Civil War took place recently enough that there is a wealth of photographs, letters, and other primary sources readily available. The Civil War was the first war in which Americans could see so much of what was happening, through photographs and newspaper accounts. Your students can experience that same information in the same way, today.

Primary sources offer a wealth of other benefits for your students as well. Textbooks often present a single interpretation of events; primary sources compel the reader to supply his or her own interpretation. A thoughtful analysis of primary sources requires these basic and advanced critical thinking skills: determining point of view; evaluating bias; classification; comparing and contrasting; and reading for detail.

Primary sources can also help students recognize that the artifacts of our contemporary lives—a ticket stub, a school report card, a yearbook—and may one day be fodder for future historians.

One of the most important steps is to help students understand the difference between primary and secondary sources. Share the chart below to demonstrate the categories to your class.

MATERIAL	DEFINITION	EXAMPLES
Primary Sources	Documents created during or immediately following the event they describe, by people who had firsthand knowledge of the event	Letters, diaries, photographs, artifacts, newspaper articles, paintings
Secondary Sources	Documents created by people who were not present at the event that occurred	History books, biographies, newspaper articles

Keep a folder handy with copies of the Primary Source Evaluation Form on page 15. Encourage students to complete this reproducible as they study each document in this book. Eventually, this kind of analysis will be automatic for your students as they encounter primary sources in their future studies.

Using the Internet to Find Primary Sources

The Internet can be an amazing tool for finding primary sources. Just remind your students that extra care has to be taken in verifying that the source is reliable. Here are a few outstanding sites for using primary sources in the classroom:

Library of Congress: **http://www.loc.gov**

National Archives and Records Administration: **http://www.nara.gov**

Internet Archive of Texts and Documents: **http://history.hanover.edu/texts.htm**

The History Place's Civil War page: **http://www.historyplace.com/civilwar/**

About American History: **http://americanhistory.about.com/cs/civilwardocument/index.htm**

Ask your students to find other great sites for primary sources and create their own list. Keep a running list handy, posted near a computer terminal.

Background on the Civil War (1861–1865)

The Civil War was the most divisive, destructive conflict in American history. More than 623,000 soldiers died on both sides. That is about the same number killed as in all other U.S. wars combined. Hundreds of thousands more were wounded. When it was over, much of the South lay in ruins.

The causes of the Civil War are varied, complex, and subject to bitter debate. For instance, saying that the Civil War was about slavery is not wrong, but it is incomplete. It was also about economics, class, and politics. These complexities present an opportunity to introduce your students to the idea that history is not clear-cut, even upon close examination.

Although the Civil War ended slavery, it did not end racism. Reconstruction was the beginning of a slow struggle that exploded, a century later, into the civil rights movement. And though the United States is much more integrated and heterogeneous than it was in the 1800s, racial and cultural issues continue to divide our people. We still wrestle with the legacy of the Civil War. The primary sources in this book will help explain why.

About this Book

The Civil War was better documented than any previous U.S. conflict. The advent of photography dovetailed with a surge in literacy. The result was an unprecedented accumulation of images, cartoons, news articles, diaries, letters, songs, and official papers. These same documents can bring the Civil War alive for your students and let them examine different points of view.

Abraham Lincoln shaped the history of our country, and two Lincoln documents are considered corner-stones of American history: the Emancipation Proclamation and the Gettysburg Address. These and other famous Civil War documents have been included along with less familiar documents that show the war through the words and images of soldiers and civilians.

Your students will benefit most from working with these sources when you help to set a context and engage them with critical viewing and thinking activities. Students can prepare for a discussion about any of the documents in this collection by studying them and completing the student reproducible Evaluate That Document! (page 18). This primary source evaluation form guides students to identify important document characteristics and pose questions prior to class discussion. Feel free to reproduce this form as you need it.

The Teaching Notes section provides background information and teaching suggestions for each document. Reproducible pages for the activity suggestions can be found at the back of the book.

Some of the documents, such as the Bill Arp column (page 35), are too difficult to read in their original form. Others, like the Alexander Stephens speech (page 21), are impossible to reproduce exactly in the way they were first experienced. So they have been typeset to make them accessible. All the documents included here should offer fresh perspectives on our nation's most troubled time.

Civil War Time Line

(1850–1865)

1850 Congress passes the Fugitive Slave Act

1851 Harriet Beecher Stowe's best-selling novel *Uncle Tom's Cabin* is published

1857 The U.S. Supreme Court hands down its Dred Scott decision declaring that slaves and free blacks are not citizens

1859 Radical abolitionist John Brown leads an unsuccessful assault on the federal arsenal at Harpers Ferry, Virginia (now West Virginia)

November 6, 1860 Abraham Lincoln is elected president of the United States

December 20, 1860 South Carolina secedes from the Union

January–February 1861 Six more states secede—Mississippi, Florida, Alabama, Georgia, Louisiana, and Texas

February 9, 1861 Jefferson Davis is elected president of the Confederate States of America at a secession convention in Montgomery, Alabama

March 4, 1861 Lincoln is inaugurated

April 12, 1861 Confederate cannons open fire on federal troops in Fort Sumter, beginning the war

April–May, 1861 Four more southern states secede—Virginia, Arkansas, Tennessee, and North Carolina—expanding the Confederacy to 11 states

April 20, 1861 Col. Robert E. Lee of Virginia resigns from the U.S. Army; he later becomes the Confederacy's top general

May 1861 Escaped slaves are employed by Union forces for the first time and declared contraband (confiscated property) of war

November 1, 1861 Gen. George B. McClellan becomes the U.S. Army commander in chief

March 9, 1862 The world's first battle between ironclad ships takes place at Hampton Roads, Virginia; the fight between the Union's *Monitor* and the Confederacy's *Merrimac* (or *Virginia*) is a draw

September 17, 1862 The Union wins the battle of Antietam in Maryland

September 22, 1862 Lincoln announces that the Emancipation Proclamation, which frees slaves in the rebelling states, will go into effect January 1, 1863

May 4, 1863 Robert E. Lee wins his most decisive victory at Chancellorsville, Virginia, but loses his best general, Thomas "Stonewall" Jackson

July 1–3, 1863 The Union wins the three-day battle of Gettysburg in Pennsylvania

July 4, 1863 Confederate forces surrender to Grant at Vicksburg, Mississippi; the Union now controls the entire Mississippi River; losses at Gettysburg and Vicksburg stagger the South

November 19, 1863 Lincoln delivers the Gettysburg Address

March 9, 1864 Lincoln makes Grant the U.S. Army's top commander

September 2, 1864 Union General William T. Sherman takes Atlanta, a vital Confederate supply center

November 8, 1864 Lincoln is reelected

March 3, 1865 The Freedman's Bureau is established

March 4, 1865 Lincoln's second inauguration is held

April 3, 1865 The Confederate capital, Richmond, Virginia, falls to Union troops

April 9, 1865 Lee surrenders to Grant at Appomattox Court House in Virginia; the war is over

April 14, 1865 Lincoln is shot by actor John Wilkes Booth and dies the next day; Andrew Johnson is sworn in as president

December 18, 1865 The 13th Amendment to the Constitution, which abolishes all slavery, goes into effect.

ANTEBELLUM ISSUES

Slaves for Sale: 1850s–1860s

Use with page 19.

BACKGROUND

Pictured here are tags assigned to slaves in Charleston, South Carolina. The tags were worn by those who were rented by their owners to other employers. Each tag listed the slave's number, skill (e.g., porter, servant, mechanic), and the year in which the tag was issued. After 1848, free blacks in Charleston also had to wear tags showing their status. Tags were used only in the Charleston area. Other marks of slave ownership, including branding, were sometimes used in the South.

This broadside announces an auction prompted by a slave owner's death. Each slave's price was determined by age, gender, skill, and the number of physical infirmities. The price also took into account what the owner paid for the slave originally. At the bottom of the poster it reads "Slaves will be sold separate, or in lots, as best suits the purchaser," indicating a willingness by the owner's heirs to split up slave families. Posters like this were common in the South.

TEACHING SUGGESTIONS

❧ Discuss with students why these artifacts are important primary source materials. What do they reveal about the time period? What do they reveal about the way enslaved people were treated? Distribute copies of the Evaluate That Document! form (page 18) and have students answer the questions for either the poster or the slave tags, drawing on the background and your discussion to further evaluate these sources.

❧ Ask students to group the slaves on the notice by age and then list the other characteristics (price and remarks about ability and disposition). What correlation do they see between age and price? What correlation between skill and price?

❧ Distribute the Civil War K-W-L Chart (page 43), and encourage students to fill in what they already know about the Civil War. Have them continue to fill in the rest of the chart as they progress through the unit.

Political Chart of the United States: 1856

Use with page 20.

BACKGROUND

From the beginning, many people in the United States were convinced that slavery was wrong, and they fought to abolish it. By the 1850s, this issue had begun to divide the country.

This chart, featuring Republican presidential candidate John C. Frémont, illustrates many of the differences between the North and the South in the antebellum (prewar) era. The Republican Party was founded in 1854, in direct response to the tensions produced by slavery. The Republican Party specifically favored banning the spread of slavery into the territories, a view held by many Northerners. In fact, one Republican slogan rallied "Free Speech, Free Press, Free Soil, Free Men, Frémont, and Victory!" Democrats countered that Frémont would cause the southern states to secede. Though he lost the 1856 presidential election to James Buchanan, Frémont won 45 percent of the northern vote total, quite an accomplishment for a political party that was only two years old.

TEACHING SUGGESTIONS

❧ Distribute copies of the Civil War Map (page 44). Have students identify the southern and northern states by shading them different colors on the map. Review the answers independently or as a group

❧ Ask students to work in small groups analyzing sections of the chart. Based on the information in their section of the chart, ask them to compare the North and the South. Ask each group to report on their section to the class and then discuss as a group what points the chart is trying to make. Ask students to decide what point of view the Republican party is taking and what other issues besides slavery the North was concerned about. Read aloud the slogan given in the background information above to confirm students' answers.

SECESSION AND WAR

Cornerstone of the Confederacy: 1861

Use with page 21.

BACKGROUND

On December 20, 1860, South Carolina seceded from the Union. The Charleston Mercury *broadside shows the announcement of the official ordinance dissolving the union.*

In February 1861, the Confederacy's Provincial Congress elected Alexander H. Stephens of Georgia as its vice president. Stephens' Cornerstone Speech was delivered at the Athenaeum in Savannah, Georgia, on March 21, 1861. Georgia and several other states had seceded, but the shelling of Fort Sumter was still about three weeks away.

In the speech, Stephens acknowledged clearly that slavery was the central tenent of the Confederacy. However, after the war, many Southerners vigorously asserted that disagreements over states' rights, not slavery, had been the main cause for secession. Ironically, Stephens himself was one of the first to make the revisionist states' rights argument following the war.

According to the Savannah Republican, *Stephens' Cornerstone speech was interrupted by cheering and applause several times. The newspaper reported that after the speech "Mr. Stephens took his seat, amid a burst of enthusiasm and applause, such as the Athenaeum has never had displayed within its walls, within 'the recollection of the oldest inhabitant.'"*

TEACHING SUGGESTIONS

⚜ Use the background above to give some context for this speech. Then either read the passage aloud yourself or have a student read it to the class. Make sure to review the meanings of difficult words such as *cornerstone* (foundation or basis) and *evanescent* (vanishing). Also, make sure students understand that slave-holding founding fathers like Washington and Jefferson mostly saw slavery as a necessary evil, not as a positive good, as Stephens does. Have students do research on the treatment of slaves by Washington, Jefferson, and other early leaders.

⚜ Discuss Stephens's points with your students. His writing style sounds somewhat archaic to modern ears, so make sure they understand what he was trying to say.

⚜ Have students look up Stephens's entire speech at **www.pointsouth.com/csanet/csa-hero.hhtm**, and click on the Cornerstone speech. Ask them to report back either in groups or individually about other points that Stephens made.

⚜ Have students do background research on Stephens. As vice president, he had a notoriously rocky relationship with Confederate President Jefferson Davis. Have them explain the feud and how it affected the southern war effort.

Songs of the War: 1860s

Use with pages 22–23.

BACKGROUND

"Dixie" became a popular hit shortly after being written by Ohioan Daniel D. Emmett in 1859. Different versions were sung by soldiers of both the North and the South, but it is the song most often associated with the South. While not an official anthem, it was played at Jefferson Davis's inaugural in 1861 and it became a battle hymn for Southern troops. Although President Lincoln asked a band at the White House to play "Dixie" after the Confederate Army's surrender in 1865, the song remains closely associated with the Confederacy, and the word "Dixie" is still shorthand for the southern U.S.

The origin of the word Dixie remains a mystery. One of the best explanations is that it originated in Louisiana, where a bank once printed $10 bills with the French word "dix," or ten, on them. People supposedly called them "dixies" and Louisiana became known as "Dix's land." The name eventually encompassed the whole South. Years after the war, the song became controversial because of the romanticized view it portrayed of the cotton-picking life of a slave, and because of the use of racist terms.

The story of "The Battle Hymn of the Republic" is more straightforward. One morning in 1861, Julia Ward Howe woke before dawn and quickly scrawled out a poem that had come to her. "The Battle Hymn of the Republic" was printed in the Atlantic Monthly *the following February. At first, it seemed to be ignored. But then Union soldiers in the camps began singing it to the tune of an already popular "Glory,*

Hallelujah." The original sheet music and lyrics are both shown on page 23. "The Battle Hymn of the Republic" became enormously popular—the most important song out of the hundreds written during the war. It remains a patriotic favorite.

TEACHING SUGGESTIONS

☙ Use the Evaluate That Document! form (page 18) to help students evaluate the lyrics to "Dixie." What are the deliberate misspellings trying to recreate? From whose point of view are they written? What story do they tell?

☙ Ask students why each of the two songs might appeal to the North or the South. What about the tune or the lyrics might have inspired each side? Note that both songs were appropriated for different uses, and had different words set to them.

☙ Have students put their research about the Civil War into verses set to the tune of "Dixie" or "The Battle Hymn of the Republic." Encourage students to include terms from the Civil War Glossary (page 46).

Wartime Photography: 1861–1864

Use with pages 24–25.

BACKGROUND

The Civil War quickly became the most photographed war in history. That's not surprising because the art of photography was still young in 1861. The first working systems of photography were not developed until the early 1840s. Cameras of the time had extremely slow shutter speeds. Some took as long as 30 seconds to snap one picture. If the subject moved at all during that time, the camera would record a blur.

"Collodian" photography was the most common type during the war. To make a picture, a photographer had to coat the plate with expensive chemicals, expose it, and develop it all within a few minutes. It was tricky, but many found ingenious ways to rig up darkrooms on wagons and in shacks or cabins—and despite all the difficulties, to take beautiful, unforgettable images.

The North had the most photographers and it had the best known: Mathew Brady. Brady was nearly blind and took few photographs himself. But he hired a stable of talented photographers whose works were

published under his name. After the war, some believed wrongly that Brady was the North's only photographer. Also, many people on both sides believed wrongly that the South had no photographers of its own.

These documents show four images taken by photographers from both sides. Each picture captures war in a way not possible before photography.

TEACHING SUGGESTIONS

☙ Have students study each picture and its caption. Guide them with questions from the Evaluate That Document! form. Ask *Why do you think the photographer took this picture? What can you tell about the people in the photo? What is special about the image?*

☙ Talk to students about obstacles that Civil War photographers had to work around such as slow shutter speeds and messy chemicals. Ask them to look at each photograph again and imagine the conditions under which it was made.

☙ Let students become photojournalists. Have them take pictures to document an event or a school assembly. Display a gallery of photographs afterward and have students write captions for their work.

☙ Ask students to discuss the effects that photography might have had on the war. Discuss how the advent of television has affected contemporary battles.

Letters Home about Soldier Life: 1864

Use with page 26.

BACKGROUND

Soldiers on both sides in the Civil War lived to get letters from home. One Union officer in Virginia wrote in March of 1865, "We have received no mail for several days and do not like it. A soldier can do without hard bread but not without his letters from home." When they had the time, supplies, and education, soldiers were prolific letter writers. Many of their letters were eloquent. Most carried requests for things like food, clothing, and more news from home. Many tried to convey to their friends and family what a soldier's life was like.

Here we have excerpts from two such

letters—one Union, one Confederate. Spelling and punctuation have been altered somewhat for clarity.

TEACHING SUGGESTIONS

✪ What kinds of inconveniences do these two soldiers talk about? How might these hardships make it more difficult to be a soldier?

✪ See if anyone in your class has had to put up with unpleasant situations while camping or hiking. Ask them about things like poison ivy, rashes, mosquitoes, carrying heavy loads, sleeping outdoors, and other difficulties. How would they have felt if they had to "rough" it for months or years on end?

✪ Distribute the Civil War Journal reproducible (page 47). Ask students to create an entry based on these letters. They can also write letters back to the soldiers.

Hospitals & the Wounded: Clara Barton: 1864

Use with page 27.

BACKGROUND

"Of all things, I'm going to avoid hospitals," one Union officer from Illinois wrote home early in the war. *"They are far more dangerous than shot and shell."* He spoke for every soldier North and South. Civil War doctors still did not understand the need for cleanliness to prevent infection and illness. They performed surgery and did their rounds in dirty, infected street clothes that spread disease. At a time when civilian hospitals were widely considered death houses, wartime hospitals could be hellish. According to one accounting, 67,000 Union soldiers died in action, but 43,000 died of wounds and 224,000 died of disease. There are no reliable figures for the Confederacy.

Army officers frequently neglected their wounded, considering it unmilitary to fuss over injured soldiers. On the other hand, many doctors, nurses, officers, and ordinary people on both sides made heroic efforts to help the sick and wounded. Clara Barton began the war as a clerk in the U.S. Patent Office. Her concern for injured soldiers soon made her a one-woman medical corps that was never formally associated with the military or any group.

After the Battle of the Wilderness in early May 1864, Barton witnessed a typical display of military callousness

toward the wounded and brought the complaint directly to a U.S. senator who pressured the War Department into action. A Union officer had refused to impose on the people of Fredericksburg, Virginia, by compelling them to house what he called "dirty, lousy, common soldiers"—his own men. Barton explained the results in her diary, which is excerpted here. Her description of the wounded men's plight is echoed in hundreds of accounts from other people on both sides of the fighting. Unfortunately, few of those accounts had such happy endings. After the war, Barton went on to found the American Red Cross in 1881.

TEACHING SUGGESTIONS

✪ Distribute the Evaluate That Document! form (page 18) and have the students read and discuss Barton's account. How might they feel if they were one of the soldiers that Barton describes?

✪ Discuss with your students the state of medical care during the Civil War. Point out that doctors did not yet know how diseases and infections were spread and only had a rough grasp on the need for cleanliness. How would such ignorance make a hospital housing hundreds of men a dangerous place?

✪ Have students research Clara Barton or Civil War medicine and report to the class.

Civil War Submarine: The C.S.S. *Hunley:* 1864

Use with page 28.

BACKGROUND

The Civil War saw many technological firsts. It was the first war in which the telegraph played a key role, the first in which large numbers of troops were moved by train, the first in which land mines were used, and the first to witness a clash of ironclad ships.

On February 17, 1864, the Civil War introduced another first: The first submarine to sink an enemy ship. The Confederate sub C.S.S. Hunley *rammed the wooden ship U.S.S.* Housatonic *just outside of Charleston Harbor in South Carolina. On the* Hunley's *ram was a long pole with a 135-pound explosive device attached. Having stuck the bomb on the* Housatonic's *hull, the* Hunley *pulled back. As it did so, the bomb went off. The Union ship sank in three minutes, killing five sailors.*

The Hunley *attacked the* Housatonic *in a failed effort to break the Federal blockade that was starving the South of badly needed food, guns, and other supplies from Europe. However, its mission was a desperate one. The* Hunley *was basically a long metal tube powered by the frantic hand-cranking of eight men. Previously, the sub had sunk twice, killing both crews. On the night it sank the* Housatonic, *the* Hunley *shined a blue light toward Charleston, signaling a successful mission. Then the sub disappeared.*

The mystery of the Hunley *was finally solved in 1995, when an underwater search team found the sub's wreck. It was lifted from 30 feet of water in 2000 and excavated. In the wreckage, researchers discovered a U.S. $20 gold coin (shown on page 28) that had been carried by the* Hunley's *last commander, Lt. George Dixon. According to family lore, a girlfriend had given Dixon the coin as a good-luck piece. While fighting at the battle of Shiloh, the coin turned out to be lucky indeed. It deflected a Yankee bullet fired at point-blank range.*

After Shiloh, Dixon had the dented coin inscribed:

Shiloh
April 6, 1862
My life Preserver
G.E.D.

TEACHING SUGGESTIONS

☙ Briefly explain the *Hunley's* story to your class. Point out to them that the two previous crews of the submarine had drowned in training. The eight men on board during its successful attack were all volunteers. Ask your students why these Confederate soldiers might have volunteered for a mission on a ship that had been so deadly?

☙ Many Civil War soldiers and sailors carried good luck pieces with them. Ask students why such items might have been so popular. Have students look at the photo showing the back of the gold coin. Can they see how it is bent from the force of the bullet? What do they think of the inscription on the back of the coin on page 28?

☙ It's still not clear why the *Hunley* sank. Did the men powering it become fatigued? Did the vessel spring a leak? Was there some other problem on board? Have your students do research into this mystery and early submarine construction.

☙ Distribute the Civil War Spy Codes reproducible (page 45). Let students work in pairs to create, send, and decode secret messages.

FROM LINCOLN'S PEN

Emancipation Proclamation: 1863

Use with pages 29–30.

BACKGROUND

Early on, Abraham Lincoln was reluctant to frame the Civil War as a crusade to free slaves, in part because he did not think he could legally take away property that was granted by the Constitution. Also, he did not want to push the four loyal, slave-holding border states—Delaware, Maryland, Kentucky, and Missouri—into the Confederacy's arms.

But his perspective changed as the war dragged on and most Northerners began to acknowledge slavery as its root cause. Also, Lincoln saw that many freed slaves wanted to serve as Union soldiers. Most important, the South's hopes hinged on winning recognition and help from England and France. Both countries wanted the South's cotton but opposed slavery. If Lincoln made freeing the South's slaves one of his war aims, neither European power would dare recognize the Confederacy.

On advice from Secretary of State William Seward, Lincoln withheld announcing the Emancipation Proclamation until the Union had scored a convincing victory. That came on September 17, 1862, at the Battle of Antietam. Five days later, Lincoln warned that slaves would be freed in all states, or parts of states, that were still in rebellion on January 1, 1863. The border states would not be affected. When that day arrived, Lincoln made good his threat. The proclamation lead to the passing of the 13th Amendment to the Constitution in 1865, which ended slavery throughout the U.S.

The broadside on page 29, a northern publication, features the text of the proclamation framed by accompanying illustrations depicting the fruits of justice brought about by the end of slavery in the South. The political cartoon on page 30 describes Lincoln, surrounded by symbols of evil and an image of a slave revolt, writing the Emancipation Proclamation. The cartoon presents the view of many Southerners at the time that the proclamation would cause social chaos and destruction.

TEACHING SUGGESTIONS

✪ Distribute the Evaluate That Document! form (page 18) to analyze this important historical document. Note that students can see many different drafts and versions of the original document in progress at the Library of Congress Web site (**www.loc.gov**), including versions in Lincoln's handwriting with his own edits.

✪ Have students examine the border illustrations in this version of the Proclamation. Viewing them from top left, around the page, what do the scenes depict? (Make sure students notice the images of the South, depicted "before" and "after" slavery.) Also point out the words in the proclamation that are bold faced and capitalized. Ask students to consider what ideas are highlighted by the different typeface treatments in the document.

✪ Ask students to compare the illustration of the broadside and the cartoon. What do the symbols and images used by the North and the South say about their different visions for the South following the proclamation?

Gettysburg Address: 1863

Use with page 31.

BACKGROUND

Only two minutes in length, the Gettysburg Address is a cornerstone document in American history. Abraham Lincoln delivered it November 19, 1863, at ceremonies dedicating the cemetery at the Gettysburg battlefield. The speech reflects Lincoln's changing thinking about the meaning of the Civil War. As historian James M. McPherson points out, Lincoln's early speeches describe the United States as a "Union." But in the Gettysburg Address the word "union" never appears. Instead, Lincoln uses the word "nation." The Gettysburg Address signals the moment that the U.S. went from being a loose aggregate of states to becoming a unified country.

Lincoln wrote five versions of the Gettysburg Address. He revised the speech even as he delivered it. For instance, the written speech he carried did not contain the phrase, "under God." As a result, there is some controversy about exactly which version Lincoln delivered. However, the fifth version is the only one he signed his name to, and it is

believed to be the most authentic.

There was some criticism of Lincoln's speech at the time. But many people recognized its brilliance right away. Several newspapers praised it. Edward Everett, the main speaker at the dedication ceremony, wrote to Lincoln: "I should be glad if I could flatter myself that I came as near to the central idea of the occasion in two hours as you did in two minutes."

TEACHING SUGGESTIONS

✪ Using the Evaluate That Document! form, ask students to determine what Lincoln was trying to accomplish with his speech. Did he succeed?

✪ Ask for several volunteers who would like to memorize and deliver the Gettysburg Address to the class. Ask them to think of the best ways to deliver the speech using eye contact, gestures, and appropriate pauses. Have other students critique these presentations constructively. Ask them which speaker was the most effective and why.

✪ The Gettysburg Address is approximately 269 words long—ask students to write speeches on a topic—chosen by you or jointly chosen as a class—and ask them to try to make their main points in 270 words.

✪ Point out to students that the Gettysburg Address was used to commemorate the first anniversary of September 11, 2001. Ask students to consider why this document was chosen to mark the occasion.

THE NORTH GAINS CONTROL

Contrabands: early 1860s

Use with page 32.

BACKGROUND

Almost as soon as Union troops marched into the South, they were besieged by runaway slaves. This was a problem because the war was officially being fought solely to preserve the Union, not to end slavery. As a result, many escaped slaves were forcibly returned by to Confederate owners by Union soldiers.

By early 1862, though, many Union officers began giving shelter to slaves as contraband of war, and soon runaways became known as "contrabands." Many of these slaves were put to work for the army as spies, scouts, laborers, and cooks. In late 1862, a few abolitionist officers formed experimental volunteer regiments made up of former slaves.

The recruiting of black soldiers became official in 1863 with Lincoln's Emancipation Proclamation. Blacks served in segregated units commanded by white officers. They received poorer medical attention and lower pay than whites (the pay issue was finally remedied retroactively by Congress). And if captured, black soldiers could expect to be killed or sold into slavery, though not all were. Nevertheless, by war's end, nearly 179,000 African Americans had enlisted and about 40,000 had died in service. The group photograph on this page shows the Band of 107th U.S. Colored Infantry at Fort Corcoran, taken at Arlington, Virginia, in 1865.

This section also highlights a contraband boy called Jackson. These two photos show his dramatic transformation from contraband to drummer boy for the 79th U.S. Colored Troops in Louisiana. We can sketch out some of the details of his life in the army: A drummer boy's main job was to keep a steady beat so that his unit could march in time. In camp, drummer boys carried water, took care of horses, ran errands, carried messages, and even cooked. During battles, they worked in hospitals, fetched ammunition, carried wounded and dead soldiers, and often became soldiers themselves.

TEACHING SUGGESTIONS

- Ask students to imagine what Jackson's life must have been like as a slave. What story do his ragged clothes tell about his owner? What do they say about how he had to live? What must it have been like to suddenly have new clothes?

- African-American soldiers battled tremendous prejudice just to be allowed to fight. One of the most famous black regiments was the 54th Massachusetts Volunteers. Its story is dramatized in the movie *Glory*. Have students either watch *Glory* or have them do research on the 54th Massachusetts and report back to the class.

"Saved Colors": 1864

Use with page 33.

BACKGROUND

On September 29, 1864, Sergeant-Major Christian Fleetwood of the 4th U.S. Colored Troops (USCT) put in his diary a three-sentence account of a battle he'd just fought in. Of his own actions, he wrote simply, "Saved colors." What he meant was that he had saved his regiment's colors from capture by the enemy. Fleetwood did not say exactly how he had done this until decades later, when he wrote a fuller description reprinted in part here. His actions that day won the attention of his superiors and a Medal of Honor—America's highest military award.

Fleetwood's memoir describes his role in the battle of Chaffin's Farm (or New Market Heights) near Richmond, Virginia. By the time that two-day battle was fought, African-American soldiers were a common sight in the Union Army. Thirteen black regiments fought at Chaffin's Farm, a Union victory. Of the 16 Medal of Honor decorations won by black soldiers in the war, 14 of them came from this one battle.

Few soldiers serving in the USCT wrote down their experiences, probably because the literacy among them was low. Fleetwood, just 23 at the time of the battle, was unusual in that he was born a free man (in Baltimore) and that he later graduated from college. His experiences at Chaffin's Farm were harrowing, and yet most combat veterans on either side could have related many similar tales.

Union regiments carried a pair of flags, or colors—a U.S. flag and a special regimental flag. Soldiers from the North and the South were encouraged to invest themselves emotionally in their colors. A unit that lost its colors to the enemy was humiliated. Being a color bearer was a high honor, but likely to be a brief one. A color bearer's prominence in battle made him an easy target.

TEACHING SUGGESTIONS

- Ask students why they think Fleetwood won a medal for his work at Chaffin's Farm. Why did picking up a flag mean so much to the men in his regiment?

- Fleetwood did not write his story down until several years after the war ended. Ask your students how that might have affected the tale he relates. What questions does he leave unanswered?

☙ Ask students to think of a dramatic event in their lives. What kinds of details do they find easy to remember? What kinds are difficult to recall? Do they think Fleetwood would have had a hard time remembering this event? Why or why not?

"Diary of a Georgia Girl" (Sherman's March): 1864

Use with page 34.

BACKGROUND

After capturing and destroying Atlanta, Union Gen. William T. Sherman embarked on the boldest, most controversial attack of the Civil War. Starting on November 16, 1864, he marched his army through Georgia's barely defended heartland in an effort to destroy the South's food, supplies, and will to fight. "If the North can march an army right through the South," he wired his friend and commander, Ulysses S. Grant, *"it is proof positive that the North can prevail."*

The South had only a 10,000-man force to face Sherman's 62,000 army. A few Confederates tried to make a stand, but Sherman simply went around or destroyed them. However, Sherman's aim was not to kill people—neither soldiers nor civilians. He wanted to destroy property that might give aid and comfort to Confederates. At this, Sherman's soldiers succeeded brilliantly. For most of them, "Sherman's March" became a rampage in which they took or demolished as much as they pleased.

Despite Southern atrocity stories, very few civilians were killed or hurt outright by Sherman's troops. Those who were killed or hurt were usually victims of Southern looters or Union "bummers"— renegades from Sherman's army. However, this was small comfort to the civilians in Sherman's path who watched their homes, valuables, and livestock brazenly destroyed or carried off. As one of Sherman's aides put it, "It is a terrible thing to see the terror and grief of these women and children."

The impotent rage Southerners felt toward Sherman is reflected in the diary of Eliza Andrews, a 24-year-old judge's daughter from Washington, Georgia. Though her own home was not directly affected, Andrews saw first-hand the miles of wasteland that the Union army left behind. The drawings show Sherman's soldiers at work tearing up the Georgia countryside.

TEACHING SUGGESTIONS

☙ Give your students background on Sherman's March and then have them read Andrews' diary entry and study these drawings using the Evaluate That Document! form (page 18). Have each student imagine that they are a Southerners caught before Sherman's army. (Note that until relatively recently, a young woman was often referred to as a "girl," as in the diary title. You might want to discuss the significance of these word choices with your students.)

☙ Then have each student take the position of a Union soldier in Sherman's army or a slave who has been liberated. How might a Northerner or a slave have responded to Andrews?

☙ On January 1, 1865, Andrews wrote in her diary: "I used to feel very brave about Yankees, but since I have passed over Sherman's track and seen what devastation they make, I am so afraid of them that I believe I should drop down dead if one of the wretches should come into my presence." Ask your students how her tone sounds different from just eight days before? Distribute the Civil War Journal (page 47) and ask students to create a journal entry that narrates how they might feel.

☙ Distribute the Civil War Map (page 44) and ask students to draw the route of Sherman's March.

Bill Arp Philosophizes Upon the War, Etc.: 1864

Use with page 35.

BACKGROUND

Bill Arp was the pen name for Charles Henry Smith (1826–1903), a writer and politician from Rome, Georgia. Smith fought as a major for the Confederate Army until receiving a medical discharge in 1863. He became famous for his Bill Arp letters, which were reprinted in newspapers throughout the South. Though Smith had a college degree, a rare and expensive item at the time, the Arp letters were written as if they came from a poor Southern farmer or backwoodsman.

Arp's homespun humor made him the South's unofficial jester. After the war, the editor of the Atlanta Constitution said that he doubted "if any papers ever produced a more thorough sensation than did the letters written by Major Smith during the war." Although his views may not have been seen as offensive at the time, they carry strongly racist connotation by today's standards.

Nevertheless, Arp was a star of Southern journalism during the war. A typical newspaper at the time was made up of one to four pages that either used a four- or eight-column format. In a four-page paper, the front page was for big news, the second page for editorials and letters like Arp's, the third and fourth pages contained ads and miscellaneous minor news stories. Because literacy was so low in the South, news stories and features like the Arp letters were often read aloud, sometimes before mass gatherings.

Reprinted here are passages from a Bill Arp letter entitled "Bill Arp Philosophizes Upon the War, Etc.," printed after Sherman's March from Atlanta to Savannah that began in November of 1864.

TEACHING SUGGESTIONS

♆ Use the Evaluate That Document! form (page 18) to consider Arp's point of view. Ask your students: What point is Arp trying to get across with the story about his mean neighbor?

♆ Arp speaks of being robbed not just by Union troops but by Confederates as well. However, he concludes that the war should go on no matter what. Ask your students to put themselves in his place. Can they imagine wanting to fight for something so badly? How might a Northerner or enslaved Southerner have responded?

Grant and Lee at Appomattox: 1865

Use with pages 36–37.

BACKGROUND

Ulysses S. Grant and Robert E. Lee are the best-known generals of the Civil War. Both made reputations for brilliant soldiering early in the war. Grant became a hero for the Union in February 1862 after capturing Fort Henry and Fort Donelson. Those victories took all of Kentucky and western Tennessee out of Confederate hands. Lee became the Confederacy's leading champion in June 1862 when he drove George B. McClellan's Army of the Potomac back from the gates of Richmond.

Much has been made of the differences between Grant and Lee. Grant was an ordinary man who, though he had attended West Point, failed at almost everything until becoming a general. Lee, on the other hand, was a wealthy Virginia aristocrat who was considered the United States' most promising soldier until he defected to the Confederacy. Some of the differences in the two men are hinted at in the cartes de visite they used. Cartes de visite were calling cards used in the 1860s by the mighty and the humble alike. People collected them in albums and especially treasured cards from famous people that had been autographed.

By April 1865, Grant and Lee had been fighting head-to-head for nearly a year. Grant suffered enormous casualties, earning him reputation as a butcher of men. But Grant, unlike the eight Union generals who had preceded him, was crushing Lee and the Confederacy. He finally trapped Lee's 35,000-man Army of Northern Virginia near Appomattox Court House in Virginia. Lee's surrender on April 9, 1865, did not end the war completely. There would still be sporadic fighting until June. But it did cause the war to end. The jubilation that followed in the North can be seen in the broadside announcing that four brutal years of fighting were over. Newspapers often published broadsides in advance of their regular editions when there was big news.

TEACHING SUGGESTIONS

♆ Distribute copies of the two *cartes de visite*. Do not tell your students who the two men are and ask those who might know to keep silent. Have students study the pictures. Ask them what they think of each man. What can they guess about each man's personality from the photo?

♆ Have your students prepare short biographies of Grant and Lee. After reading them aloud, have the students contrast their personalities. Does what they found jibe with their impressions from the *cartes de visite?* Which man was the better general?

♆ Encourage students to read more about the history of *cartes de visite*. These two come from the album of John Hay, one of Lincoln's secretaries. Students can peruse the album online by visiting: **memory.loc.gov/ammem/ cwphome.html** and clicking on "Civil War photograph album."

U Have students read the broadside announcing Lee's surrender. What do the letters quoted in the broadside discuss? Why is the language of both letters so cautious? This broadside shows how Northerners felt. How might people in the South have taken the news?

AFTERMATH

Lincoln's Assassination: 1865

For use with page 38.

BACKGROUND

The famous actor John Wilkes Booth, a Southern sympathizer, shot Abraham Lincoln on April 14, 1865, at Ford's Theater in Washington, D.C. At the time, Lincoln carried two pairs of spectacles (one repaired with a piece of string where the screw had been); a lens polisher; a pocketknife; a watch fob; and a brown leather wallet holding a five-dollar Confederate note as well as nine newspaper clippings. The clippings (not shown in the photograph on page 38) included several with positive things to say about Lincoln and his policies. When Lincoln died on the morning of April 15 (at age 56), these personal effects were given to his son Robert Lincoln. The Library of Congress acquired them from a granddaughter of Lincoln in 1937. Included with the artifacts is an April 15, 1965 front page from The New York Herald *that carries the report of Lincoln's assassination.*

Usually the Library of Congress does not keep personal affects among its holdings, and these items were not put on display until 1976. The Librarian of Congress at the time they were donated believed that a display of such mundane personal effects might lessen Lincoln's "god-like" status among Americans. However, this exhibit is a favorite.

TEACHING SUGGESTIONS

U Have students spread the contents of their own pockets out on a table. What might those items tell other people? What sorts of questions or impressions do students form based on the contents of Lincoln's pockets? Why might he have been

carrying newspaper articles in his wallet? Why the five-dollar Confederate bill?

U Have students compare the *New York Herald* front page layout to that of a newspaper today. How are words, spaces, and typefaces in the titles and subheads used to attract attention and convey information about the assassination? How might the same information be conveyed today? Students can compare this document with a current front page article about a catastrophe or with the headlines announcing President Kennedy's assassination on November 22, 1963.

The Freedman's Second Reader: 1865

For use with page 39.

BACKGROUND

On March 3, 1865, Congress established a temporary agency called the Bureau of Refugees, Freedmen, and Abandoned Lands. Everybody soon called it the Freedman's Bureau. It was designed to help the more than 4 million former slaves adjust to their new lives. O.O. Howard, a Union general famous for his Christian piety, was named its one and only commissioner.

The Bureau wore many hats. It helped set fair wages for black laborers and helped black farmers obtain land. It served as a court system for resolving disputes and often intervened on behalf of ex-slaves who were threatened with persecution. It registered thousands of black voters and helped an estimated 500,000 freed slaves get medical care.

The Bureau's most lasting impact came in the area of education. It helped Northern relief groups like American Freedman's Union Commission to found schools. By 1869, more than 3,000 schools served more than 150,000 pupils. The Bureau also helped create the first black universities in the South. This exercise shows a page from "The Freedman's Second Reader," a textbook prepared for freedmen by Northern reformers.

In many ways, the Freedman's Bureau was a heartbreaking failure. There was corruption among its 900 or so agents. Also, it's defense of and help for freedmen was often tepid. However, the educational opportunities it provided helped pave the way for future civil rights victories.

TEACHING SUGGESTIONS

❂ Use the Evaluate That Document! form (page 18) to guide students as they study this document. Explain to your students that slaves had been prohibited by law and custom from learning how to read or write. Ask them why white slave owners might have wanted to keep their slaves uneducated. When freedmen's schools were created after the war, thousands of ex-slaves anxiously attended. Why would education have been so important to them?

❂ Explain to your students that black families were often broken up by slave auctions and by the whims of masters. Given that, why does this textbook page use the theme of a "model" black household? What is the paragraph intended to show about how freedmen should live?

❂ After the war, many (though certainly not all) ex-Confederates tried to keep blacks from going to school. Books and buildings were burned, students and teachers (both white and black) were harassed or killed. Why would white Southerners want to keep freed blacks ignorant?

❂ Have your students do research on O.O. Howard and the Freedman's Bureau. What did Howard and the Bureau accomplish? Why did they not accomplish more?

A Picture of the Desolated States: 1865–1866

Use with pages 40–42.

BACKGROUND

In the summer of 1865 and the following winter, Northern writer J.T. Trowbridge (1827–1916) made two trips through the defeated South. He visited old battlefields, farms, and burnt-out cities. He spoke to plantation owners, ex-slaves, Union officers, and anyone else who could give him insight into the post-war South.

Trowbridge was an abolitionist who, like many Northerners of the time, harbored great anger toward the South over the war. Nevertheless, he wanted to find out how Southerners felt and report back to other Northerners. The result was a book called A Picture of the Desolated States.

At the time of Trowbridge's two visits, feelings from the "late unpleasantness" were still very raw in the South. Union troops occupied all 11 of the rebellious states. President Andrew Johnson and Congress were already bickering over how to handle Reconstruction. Nobody was sure how or if the divided country would reunite.

First published in 1866, Trowbridge's book bluntly favored a hard Reconstruction and complete civil rights for ex-slaves. But he let the voices of Southerners—both white and black—come through in his writing. "[This book] is a record of actual observations and conversations," he wrote in the introduction, "free from fictitious coloring."

TEACHING SUGGESTIONS

❂ Give your students some background on Trowbridge's book. Then distribute copies of the Evaluate That Document! form (page 18) and have them read the excerpts and study the accompanying photographs. Which of the incidents hits them the strongest? Are any of them surprising? Why?

❂ Ask students whether they consider Trowbridge's book "free from fictitious coloring" as the author describes it. Does representing different viewpoints contribute to his credibility? Also have them consider which quotes show signs of bitterness. Why do they think the bitterness is there? Who is it directed at? Is it justified? Which quotes show some sign of hope or reconciliation?

❂ As Trowbridge's book was being written, the Ku Klux Klan and other nightrider groups were being formed by white Southerners. What hints of this development do students see in these quotes?

❂ Have your students do research on the Reconstruction era. What was it? How long did it last? What did it accomplish? There are still sharp differences of opinion about how it was carried out. What are they? Have them report back to the class.

Evaluate That Document!

Title or name of document _____

Date of document _____

Type of document:

❑ letter   ❑ patent

❑ diary/journal   ❑ poster

❑ newspaper article   ❑ advertisement

❑ photograph   ❑ drawing/painting

❑ map   ❑ cartoon

❑ telegram   ❑ other _____

Point of view:

Who created this document? _____

For whom was this document created? _____

_____

What was the purpose for creating this document? _____

_____

What might the person who created it have been trying to express? _____

_____

What are two things you can learn about the time period from this primary source?

_____

_____

What other questions do you have about this source?

_____

_____

_____

_____

_____

_____

SLAVES FOR SALE

Slave tags: 1857, 1863

	Name.	Age.	Qualification.
	Andrew,	46	
	Sue,		
690	Dick,		
	Bella,		
	Martha,		
6	Hester,		
435	Sary,		
	Billy,		
	Caroline,		
4	Jacob,		
	Nanny Miles,		
700	Elijah,		
3	Liddy,		
	Jim,		
1130	Phœbe,		
3	Flora,		
	Paris,		
450	Lizzy,		
2			
	Quincy,		
750	Abel,		
3	Alfred,		
	Bob,		
	Margaret,		
510	Dean,		
	Cilla,		
5	Sambo,		
	Wally,		
	Sue,		
650	Robert,		
	Patty,		
5	Rhoda,		
580	Jeffry,	1	
225	Monday,	1	
	Catharina,		
615	Harry,	2	
	Jack,		
	Kate,		
660	Alice,		
4	Elizabeth,		
	Fortune,		
	Maria,		
650	Jane,		
4	Gloe,		
760	Julius,	1	These th to a city to remain
	Louisa,		
2	Clyde,		

	Name.	Age.	Qualification.
285	London,	60	Excellent driver.
2	Rhina,	50	
	Anthony,	32	Excellent carpenter.
	Maria,	27	
	Diana,	6	
	Betsy,	4	
600 5	Hager,	3 mos.	Infant.
	Sharper,	45	
	Nelly,	44	
	Sally,	18	
	Molly,	16	
600 5	Nelly,	3 mos.	Infant.
	Patty,	60	
570	Eliza,	32	
3	Young Patty,	15	
	Ned,	55	
	Auba,	50	
	Jacob,	20	
500	Eliza,	18	
	Mack,	8	
6	Anthony,	6 mos.	Infant.
	Hector,	45	
410	Grace,	40	
3	Hannah,	4	
610	Jack Broughton,	65	
2	Mingo,	21	
	Peggy,	30	
	Charles,	10	
405	Sharper,	4	
	Cyrus,	3	
	Harry,	6 mos.	Infant.
6	Old Juno,	70	
	October,	65	
275	Bella,	60	
	Elsey,	22	
4	Old Jack Wilson,	76	
	Nann,	45	
	Ben,	20	
620	Rose,	18	
4	Old Maria,	65	
	Mary Ann,	60	
760	Prince,	18	
3	Hager,	15	
	Israel,	60	Boatman and field hand.
	Tilla,	50	Nurse.
	Willoughby,	18	
415	Rose,	25	
	William,	5	
	Robert,	2	
7	Tilla,	5 mos.	Infant.
	Sumner,	35	Boatman and field hand.
710	Eady,	25	
	Juba,	22	
4	Thomas,	7 mos.	Infant.
	Jeffry,	40	Excellent carpenter,
	Patty,	35	
650	William,	14	
	George,	10	
	Maria,	3	
6	Jeffry,	18 mos.	Infant.

UNDER DECREE IN EQUITY.

Ex-parte,

WINTHROP & ROSE, Trustees.

WILL BE SOLD ON

Tuesday, 31st day of January, 1860,

AT ELEVEN O'CLOCK, A. M., AT THE

MART IN CHALMERS STREET,

UNDER THE DIRECTION OF

JAMES TUPPER, Master in Equity,

A VERY

PRIME AND ORDERLY GANG

OF

ONE HUNDRED AND SIX NEGROES.

TERMS.

One-third Cash, balance in one and two years, secured by bond, mortgage, and two approved sureties.

CHARLESTON, S. C.
WALKER, EVANS & CO., PRINTERS, 3 BROAD STREET.

Auction notice: 1852

POLITICAL CHART OF THE UNITED STATES
1856

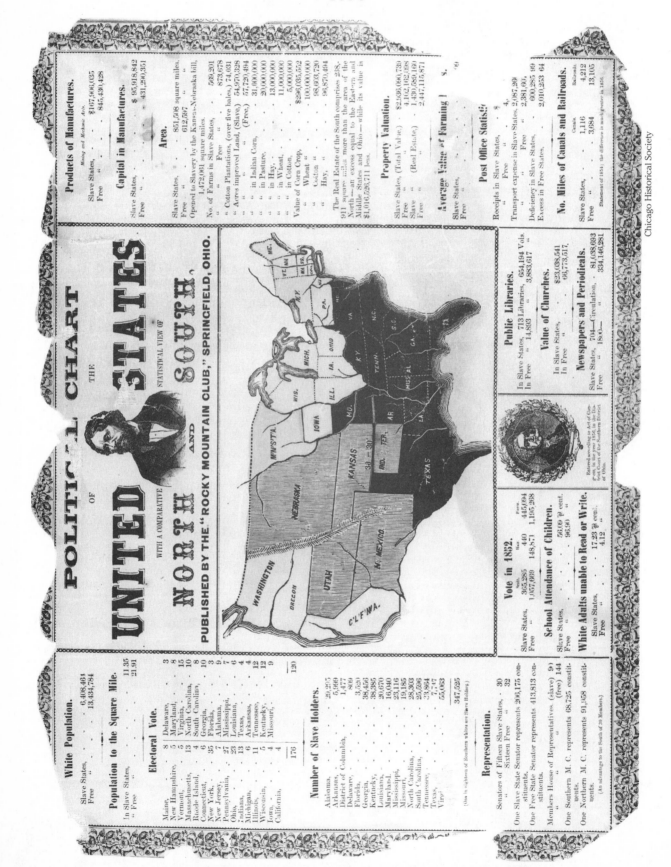

Chicago Historical Society

CORNERSTONE OF THE CONFEDERACY
1861

National Archives

"The prevailing ideas entertained by [Thomas Jefferson] and most of the leading statesmen at the time of the formation of the [U.S.] Constitution were, that the enslavement of the African was in violation of the laws of nature; that it was wrong in principle, socially, morally, and politically.

It was an evil they knew not well how to deal with; but the general opinion of the men of that day was that, somehow or other, in the order of Providence, the institution would be evanescent and pass away. . . . Those ideas, however, were fundamentally wrong. They rested upon the assumption of the equality of the races. This was an error. It was a sandy foundation, and the idea of a government built upon it fell when the 'storm came and the wind blew.'

"Our new Government is founded upon exactly the opposite idea; its foundations are laid, its cornerstone rests upon the great truth that the negro is not equal to the white man; that slavery— subordination to the superior race— is his natural and moral condition. This, our new government, is the first, in the history of the world, based upon this great physical, philosophical, and moral truth. . . ."

—*Confederate Vice President Alexander Stephens gave this speech on March 21, 1861, in Savannah, Georgia*

CHARLESTON
MERCURY
EXTRA:

Passed unanimously at 1.15 o'clock, P. M. December 20th, 1860.

AN ORDINANCE

To dissolve the Union between the State of South Carolina and other States united with her under the compact entitled "The Constitution of the United States of America."

We, the People of the State of South Carolina, in Convention assembled, do declare and ordain, and it is hereby declared and ordained,

That the Ordinance adopted by us in Convention, on the twenty-third day of May, in the year of our Lord one thousand seven hundred and eighty-eight, whereby the Constitution of the United States of America was ratified, and also, all Acts and parts of Acts of the General Assembly of this State, ratifying amendments of the said Constitution, are hereby repealed; and that the union now subsisting between South Carolina and other States, under the name of "The United States of America," is hereby dissolved.

THE
UNION
is
DISSOLVED!

Library of Congress

SONGS OF THE WAR

"Dixie's Land"—1859

Verse 1

I wish I was in de land ob cotton,
Old times dar am not forgotten,

Look away, Look away!
Look away! Dixie Land.

In Dixie Land whar I was born
  in,
Early on one frosty morning,

Look away, Look away!
Look away! Dixie Land.

Chorus

Den i wish I was in Dixie,
Hooray! Hooray!

In Dixie Land, I'll took my stand,
To lib and die in Dixie.

Away, away, away down south in
  Dixie.
Away, away, away down south in
  Dixie.

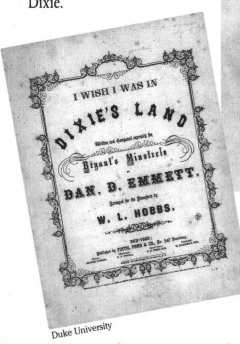

Duke University

SONGS OF THE WAR

"Battle Hymn of the Republic"—1861

BATTLE HYMN OF THE REPUBLIC.

BY MRS. JULIA WARD HOWE.

Mine eyes have seen the glory of the coming of the Lord:
He is trampling out the vintage where the grapes of wrath
    are stored ;
He hath loosed the fateful lightnings of His terrible swift sword:
        His truth is marching on.
    Chorus—Glory, glory, hallelujah !
        Glory, glory, hallelujah !
        Glory, glory, hallelujah !
            His truth is marching on.

I have seen Him in the watch-fires of a hundred circling camps ;
They have builded Him an altar in the evening dews and
    damps :
I can read His righteous sentence by the dim and flaring lamps :
        His day is marching on.
    Chorus—Glory, glory, hallelujah, &c.
            His day is marching on.

I have read a fiery gospel writ in burnished rows of steel :
" As ye deal with my contemners, so with you my grace shall
    deal ;
Let the Hero, born of woman, crush the serpent with his heel,
        Since God is marching on."
    Chorus—Glory, glory, hallelujah &c.
            Since God is marching on.

He has sounded forth the trumpet that shall never call retreat ;
He is sifting out the hearts of men before His judgment seat :
Oh, be swift, my soul, to answer Him ! be jubilant my feet !
        Our God is marching on !
    Chorus—Glory, glory, hallelujah, &c.
            Our God is marching on !

In the beauty of the lilies Christ was born across the sea,
With a glory in His bosom that transfigures you and me ;
As he died to make men holy, let us die to make men free,
        While God is marching on.
    Chorus—Glory, glory, hallelujah, &c.
            While God is marching on.

Published by the Supervisory Committee for Recruiting Colored Regiments

Library of Congress

Duke University

WARTIME PHOTOGRAPHY
1861–1864

U.S. Army Military History Institute

Group portraits like this 1861 shot were one of the most common types of wartime photo. This one shows men from the Washington Artillery of New Orleans, a unit in the Confederate army. This type of group portrait would have been unthinkable before photography. Paintings and drawings were too expensive for all but the rich to afford. What can you tell about these men by looking at them?

Taking a bath was a rare treat for men on either side of the war. These are Union soldiers swimming in the North Anna River near Fredericksburg, Virginia, in May of 1864. This picture shows one of the problems of Civil War photographs. Two of the swimmers moved while the picture was being taken, so their images are blurry.

Library of Congress

This famous photograph of a dead Rebel was taken just after the Battle of Gettysburg in July of 1863. The photographer moved the body 40 yards and positioned the rifle to make a more dramatic image. Does knowing that change your opinion of the photo? Such posing was a common practice among photographers. Do you think it was right?

Library of Congress

Library of Congress

This is the rarest type of all Civil War photos—one that shows combat. A Confederate photographer took it in September of 1863 at Fort Sumter in Charleston, South Carolina. He luckily snapped the photo as a Union shell blew up in the middle of the fort. In the lower left-hand corner you can see blurry images of Confederate soldiers. Like many photos taken during the war, this one has faded badly. What details can you make out?

LETTERS HOME ABOUT SOLDIER LIFE
1864

Private John F. Brobst
[Union Soldier]
25th Wisconsin Infantry
Spring 1864

It is very hard to be a soldier. No matter how bad the weather is you must go. If it rains you must stand or sleep out, with not as much as a leaf to shelter you from the storm. Perhaps have about half a meal for two days, and that the poorest kind of living . . . . This is not the case at all times, for when we are where we can get it we have plenty, and that which is good. But most of the time we are on the move and then we cannot get such as is fit for a man to eat.

Now, I will tell you as near as I can what the load is that a soldier has to carry, and march from 15 to 25 miles a day. He as a gun that weighs 11 pounds, cartridges and cartridge box about 6 pounds, woolen blanket 3 pounds, canteen full of water which they oblige you to keep full all the time, which is about 6 pounds, then three or five days' rations, which will weigh about 8 pounds, and then your little trinkets that we need, perhaps 2 pounds, makes a total of about 45 or 50 pounds. That is what makes us think of our homes in these hot days.

Union soldier, 1861

Lieutenant John W. Comer
[Confederate Soldier]
45th Alabama Infantry
June 14, 1864

"I am glad to say that I am still safe & well. I never enjoyed better health in my life, I have a few sores on one of my feet, caused I think from such hard and continual marching. We have been on the [march] since . . . the 5th day of May. When we lie down at night we do not know how long we will be permitted to sleep, all the principle maneuvers are made in the night. I never think of pulling off my clothes or shoes when I lie down. I have not pulled off my pants or shoes to lie down more than twice since the 5th of May. I sleep with my belt around me & my sword & haversack under my head so as to be ready to move in a moment when called upon. . . . I do not believe there is a soldier in this army but what has got lice (body lice I mean). I have got my clothes boiled [to get rid of the lice] but to no purpose. . . . They plague me half to death, keeping me scratching & feeling . . . While I am writing our pickets [advanced sentries] are fighting in front & the enemy are cannonading heavily. But I have become accustomed to the sound and it does not bother me at all. . . .

Lt. [John] Wallace Comer,
and Burrell, his 'body servant'

HOSPITALS AND THE WOUNDED:
CLARA BARTON

1864

Atlanta History Center

"I saw crowded into one old sunken hotel, lying helpless upon its bare, wet, bloody floors, five hundred fainting men hold[ing] up their cold, bloodless, dingy hands as I passed, and beg[ging] me in Heaven's name for a cracker to keep them from starving (and I had none); or to give them a cup that they might have something to drink water from, if they could get it (and I had no cup and could get none); till I saw two hundred six-mule army wagons in a line, ranged down the street to headquarters, and reaching so far out on the Wilderness road that I never found the end of it; every wagon crowded with wounded men, stopped, standing in the rain and mud, wrenching back and forth by the restless, hungry animals all night from four o'clock in the afternoon till eight next morning and how much longer I know not. The dark spot in the mud under many a wagon, told only too plainly where some poor fellow's life had dripped out in those dreadful hours. . . .

> Barton rushed to Washington to get the help from Sen. Henry Wilson, the chairman of a powerful Senate committee. Wilson, in turn, went to the War Department to get some action. Instead, officials there hemmed and hawed and said Wilson's information must be incorrect.

. . . Mr. Wilson assured them that the officers [at Fredericksburg] were not to be relied upon. . . . Still the Department doubted. It was then that he proved that my confidence in his firmness was not misplaced, as, facing his doubters he replies: "One of two things will have to be done—either you will send someone tonight with the power to investigate and correct the abuses of our wounded men at Fredericksburg, or the Senate will send someone tomorrow."

This threat recalled their scattered senses. . . .

. . . At two o'clock in the morning the Quartermaster-General and staff [headed off to Fredericksburg]. At noon the wounded men were fed from the food of the city and the houses were opened to the 'dirty, lousy soldiers' of the Union Army. . . .

Both railroad and canal were opened. In three days I returned with carloads of supplies.

CIVIL WAR SUBMARINE:
C.S.S. *Hunley*

1864

Museum of the Confederacy

Gold Coin Artifact

Friends of the Hunley, Inc.

EMANCIPATION PROCLAMATION
1863

Northern View

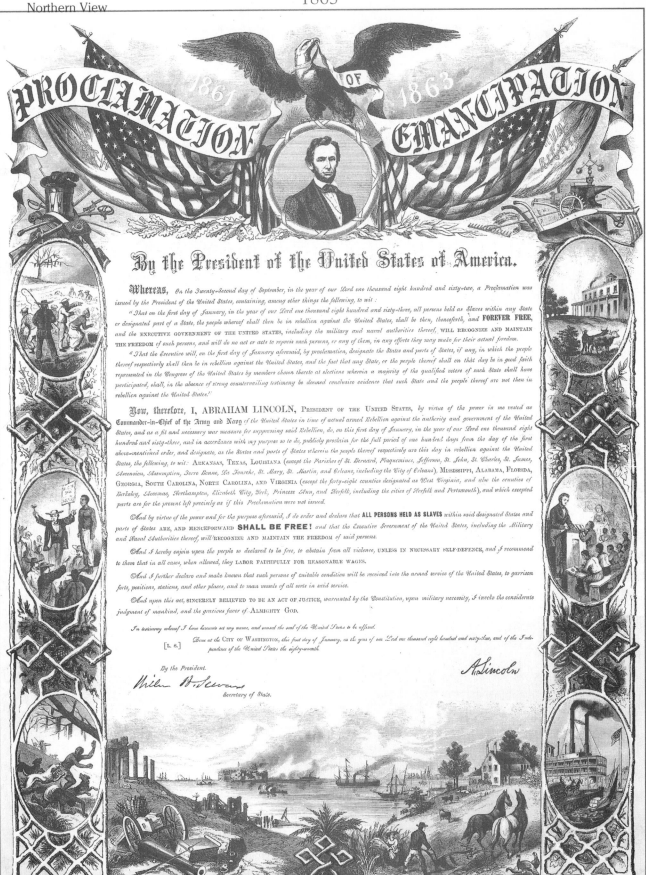

EMANCIPATION PROCLAMATION
1863

Southern View

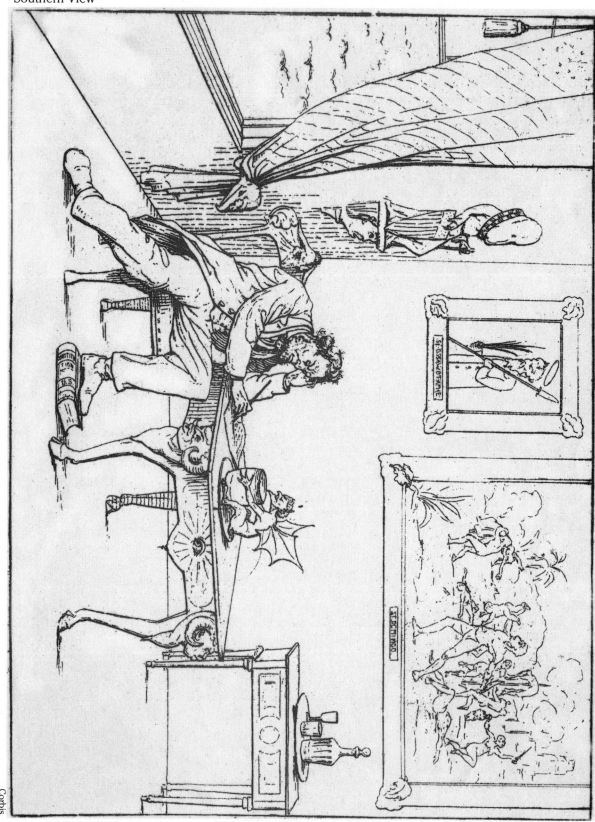

Corbis

GETTYSBURG ADDRESS

1863

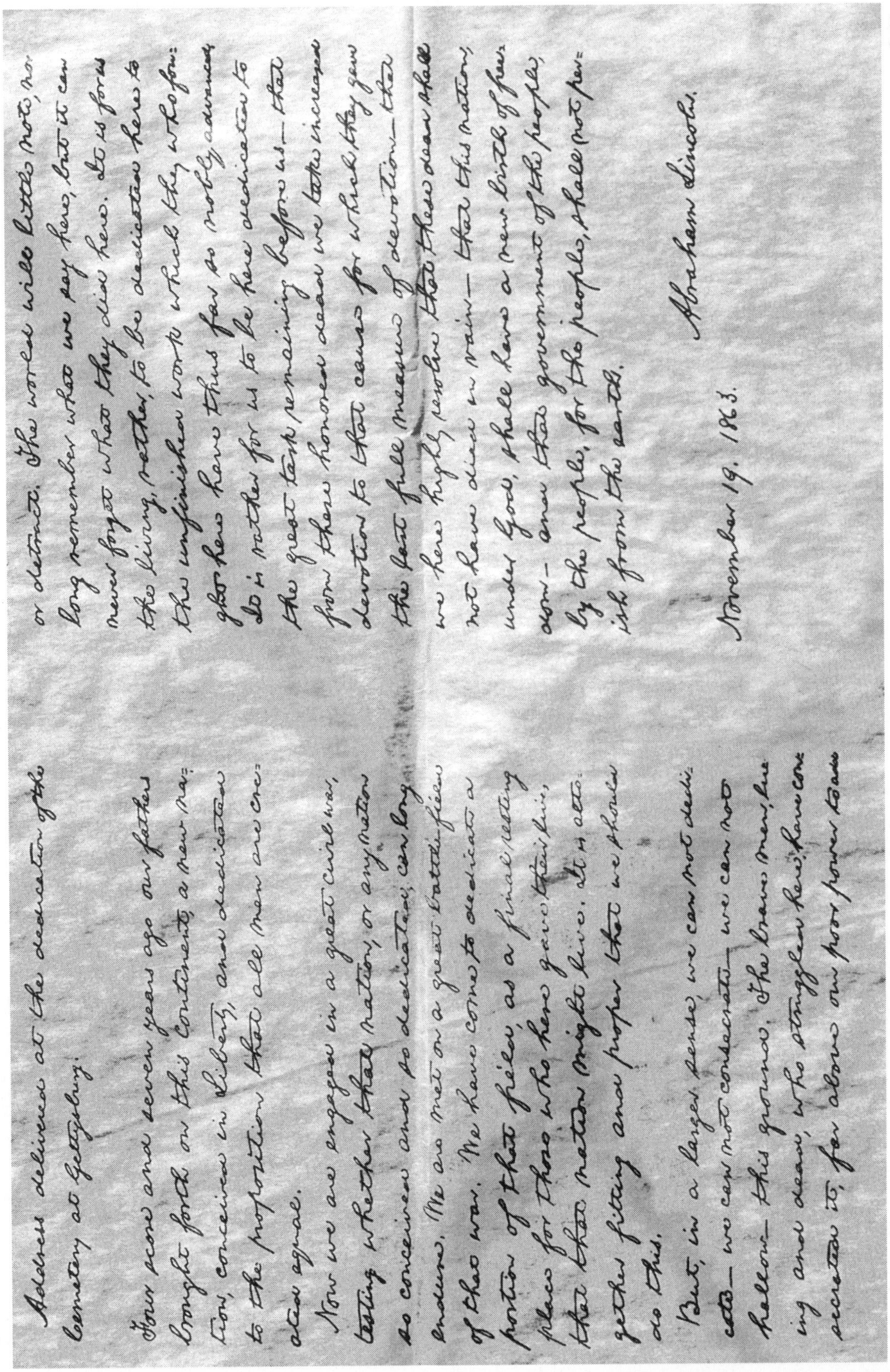

Address delivered at the dedication of the
Cemetery at Gettysburg.

Four score and seven years ago our fathers
brought forth on this continent, a new nation, conceived in Liberty, and dedicated
to the proposition that all men are created equal.

Now we are engaged in a great civil war,
testing whether that nation, or any nation
so conceived and so dedicated, can long
endure. We are met on a great battle-field
of that war. We have come to dedicate a
portion of that field, as a final resting
place for those who here gave their lives
that that nation might live. It is alto-
gether fitting and proper that we should
do this.

But, in a larger sense, we can not dedicate — we can not consecrate — we can not
hallow — this ground. The brave men, living and dead, who struggled here, have con-
secrated it, far above our poor power to add
or detract. The world will little note, nor
long remember what we say here, but it can
never forget what they did here. It is for us
the living, rather, to be dedicated here to
the unfinished work which they who fought here have thus far so nobly advanced.
It is rather for us to be here dedicated to
the great task remaining before us — that
from these honored dead we take increased
devotion to that cause for which they gave
the last full measure of devotion — that
we here highly resolve that these dead shall
not have died in vain — that this nation,
under God, shall have a new birth of free-
dom — and that government of the people,
by the people, for the people, shall not per-
ish from the earth.

November 19. 1863.

Abraham Lincoln.

Corbis

CONTRABANDS
early 1860s

"Before" and "after" photographs of Jackson, an escaped slave enlisted as a drummer boy in the Union army. Such enlistment was illegal or *contraband* before the signing of the Emancipation Proclamation.

Corbis

Corbis

Band of the 107th Colored Infantry

Library of Congress

"SAVED COLORS"

1864

On September 29, 1864, Sergeant-Major Christian A. Fleetwood was one of 350 black enlisted men and eleven white officers in the 4th U.S. Colored Troops who charged Confederate earthworks (dug-out trenches and built-up embankments for fighting) at the Battle of Chaffin's Farm. Only about 115 enlisted men and three officers returned from the charge. The others were killed or wounded. Here is Fleetwood's account:

"It was a deadly hailstorm of bullets, sweeping men down as hailstones sweep the leaves from the trees, and it was not long before [the second flag-bearer] also went down, shot through the leg. As he fell he held up the flags and shouted: 'Boys, save the colors!'

Corbis

"Before they could touch the ground, Corporal Charles Veal, of Company D, had seized the blue [regimental] flag, and I the American flag, which had been presented to us by the patriotic women of our home in Baltimore.

"It was very evident that there was too much work cut out for our regiments. Strong earthworks, protected in front by two lines abatis *[network of cut-down trees]* and one line of palisades *[sharpened sticks]*, and in the rear by a lot of men who proved that they knew how to shoot and largely outnumbered us. We struggled through the two lines of abatis, a few getting through the palisades, but it was sheer madness, and those of us who were able had to [retreat] as best we could....

"I have never been able to understand how Veal and I lived under such a hail of bullets, unless it was because we were both such little fellows. I think I weighed then about 125 pounds and Veal about the same. We did not get a scratch. A bullet passed between my legs, cutting my bootleg, trousers, and even my stocking, without breaking the skin."

"DIARY OF A GEORGIA GIRL"

1864

"December 24, 1864. —About three miles from Sparta [Georgia] *we struck the 'burnt country,' as it was well named by the natives, and then I could better understand the wrath and desperation of these poor people. I almost felt as if I should like to hang a Yankee myself. There was hardly a fence left standing all the way from Sparta to Gordon. The fields were trampled down and the road lined with carcasses of horses, hogs, and cattle that the invaders, unable either to consume or carry away with them, had wantonly shot down, to starve out the people and prevent them from making their crops. The stench in some places was unbearable; every few hundred yards we had to hold our noses or stop them with the cologne Mrs. Elzey had given us, and it proved a great* [benefit]. *The dwellings that were standing all showed signs of pillage, and on every plantation we saw the charred remains of the ginhouse and packing screw* [where cotton was prepared for market], *while here and there lone chimney stacks, 'Sherman's sentinels,' told of homes laid in ashes. The infamous wretches!"*

—Eliza Andrews, a wealthy 24-year-old Georgian traveling in the wake of Sherman's March

University of NC at Chapel Hill

Bettman/Corbis

BILL ARP PHILOSOPHIZES
UPON THE WAR, ETC.

1864

Late in the war, Bill Arp (the pen name of Charles Henry Smith) encouraged southerners to fight on in spite of their mounting losses on the battlefield.

University of NC at Chapel Hill

"My doctrine has always been, that if we was to fight and fight and fight until our army was played out, the biggest part of old Lincoln's job would be just begun. After he has whipped us, then he has got to subjugate us. He has got to hold us down, and he can't do it.

"I used to have a neighbor who was one of these mean, little, snarling [ornery dog] sort of men, and I had him to whip about once a week for three months, but I didn't make a thing off of him. He would raise a new fuss with me in an hour after I had made him holler enough, and finally I sold him my land, and moved away just to get rid of him.

"Now the idea of old Lincoln taking possession of so many towns and cities, and so much territory, and holding it and keeping so many people down, is utter nonsense, and it can't be done. Besides, we are not whipped yet – not by three or four jug fulls.

"Suppose Sherman did walk right through the State. Suppose he did. Was anybody whipped? Didn't the rebellion just close right up on the ground behind him . . . . He parted the atmosphere as he went along, and it collapsed again in his rear immediately. He will have to go over that old ground several times yet, and then sell out and move away."

Arp also expressed the frustrations of fellow southerners when he made fun of the Confederate Army and Confederate politicians.

"What the Yankees didn't get in six months' continuous plunder, was brought out to enjoy when they left. Suddenly some friendly scouts appeared upon the arena, and made a general grab. Everything visible was appropriated without pay or ceremony. Our indignant citizens appealed for protection, and his Excellency the Governor sent up a Major as the avenger of our wrongs, and the protector of our lives and property. The Major and his gallant boys appreciated our cause, and in order to prevent a recurrence of such robberies by the wandering scouts, they stole all the balance themselves and then run away. Such is war, Mr. Editor, but nevertheless, notwithstanding, I am for it as long as possible, and longer if necessary."

GRANT AND LEE AT APPOMATTOX
1865

Cartes de Visite
(calling cards)

Library of Congress

Library of Congress

Glory to God in the Highest: Peace on
Earth, Good will amongst men.

E PLURIBUS UNUM

EXTRA DISPATCH.

LEE'S SURRENDER ¡

FULL PARTICULARS.

Correspondence between Gens. Grant & Lee.

The Army of Northern Virginia Surrendered !!

The following correspondence concerning the most important event of the war, explains itself. It was dispatched to Gen. Pope from Was'ti gton this morning:

WASHINGTON, D. C., April 9, 1865.
To Maj. Gen DODGE:

This Department has just received the official report of the surrender this day of Gen. Lee and his army to Lieut General Grant, on the terms proposed by General Grant. Details will be given as speedily as possible   Signed

E. M. STANTON,
Sec'y. of War.

HEADQ'RS ARMY OF UNITED STATES, }
April 9, 1865 P M. }

To Hon. E. M. Stanton, Sec'y of War :

General Lee surrendered the Army of Northern Virginia this afternoon upon terms proposed by myself. The accompanying and additional correspondence will show the conditions fully.

(Signed)   U. S. GRANT,
Lieut. General.

April 9, 1865.—General: I received your note of this morning on the picket line, whither I had come to meet you to ascertain definitely what terms were embraced in your propositions of yesterday with reference to the surrender of this army.

I now request an interview, in accordance with the offer contained in your letter of yesterday, for that purpose.

Very resp'y, Your ob't. s'vt.,
(Signed),   R. E. LEE, Gen.

To Lt. Gen. U. S. Grant, Com'dg U. S A.
Your note of this date, is but this moment, 11:50 A. M. received. In consequence of my having passed from the Richmond and Lynchburg road, to the Farmville and Lynchburg I am thus writing about four miles of Walters Church and will push forward to the front for the purpose of meeting you. Notice sent to me on this road where you

wish the interview to take place will meet me.

Very respectfully,
Your obedient servant,

U. S. GRANT, Lt. General.
APPOMATTOX COURT HOUSE, April 9, '65.

GENERAL R. E. LEE, Com'dg C. S. A. :

In accordance with the substance of my letter to you of the 8th inst , I propose to receive the surrender of the Army of Northern Virginia on the following terms, to-wit: Rolls of all the officers and men to be made in duplicate, one copy to be given to an officer designated by me, the other to be retained by such officer or officers as you may designate.

The officers to give their individual paroles not to take up arms against the Government of the United States, until properly exchanged, and each company or regimental commander sign a like parole for the men of their commands. The arms, artillery and public property to be parked or stacked, and turned over to the officers appointed by me to receive them. This will not embrace the side arms of the officers.

This done, such officer and men will be allowed to return to their homes, not to be disturbed by U. S. authority so long as they observe their paroles and the laws in force where they may reside.

Very respectfully,
U. S. GRANT, Lt. Gen.

H'DQRS. ARMY OF NORTHERN VA.,
April 9, 1865.

Lt. Gen. U. S. Grant, Com'dg. U. S. A.

General: I have received your letter of this date containing the terms of surrender of the Army of Northern Virginia, as proposed by you. As they are substantially the same as those expressed in your letter of the 8th inst., they are accepted.

I will proceed to designate the proper officers to carry the stipulations into effect.

Very Resp'y, Your Ob't. S'vt,
R. E. LEE, Gen.

Further particulars in first Edition Evening Dispatch.

LINCOLN'S ASSASSINATION
1865

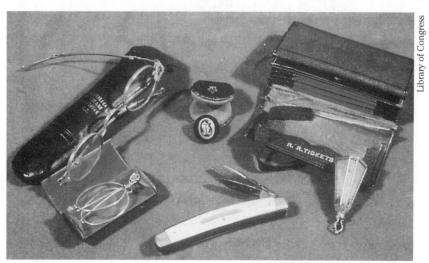

Articles found in President Lincoln's pockets on April 14, 1865.

A FREEDMAN'S SECOND READER
1865

SECOND READER.   35

LESSON XV.

cock	wash	pig	too
crows	dawn	dig	two
food	bound	hoe	scrub
wake	clean	plow	bake
home	know	noise	eyes
cheer	knives	kneel	school

What letter is silent in hoe? in clean? Say just, not *jist* catch, not *cotch*; sit, not *set*; father, not *fuder*.

THE FREEDMAN'S HOME.

SEE this home! How neat, how warm, how full of cheer, it looks! It seems as if the sun shone in there all the day long. But it takes more than the light of the sun to make a home bright all the time. Do you know what it is? It is love.

A Picture of the Desolated States

1865–1866

Following the war, Northern writer J.T. Trowbridge toured the South and recorded the reflections of the people he met. Excerpts from his book follow. At the old Antietam battlefield in Maryland, Trowbridge found a graveyard for both Union and Confederate soldiers that had been dug up by a farmer's hogs.

Library of Congress

Graves of Confederate soldiers in Hollywood Cemetery, VA, 1865.

"I picked up a skull lying loose on the ground like a cobblestone. It was that of a young man; the teeth were all splendid and sound. How hideously they grinned at me! And the eye sockets were filled with dirt. . . . I turned the skull in my hand, half-regretting that I could not carry it away with me. My first shuddering aversion to the grim relic was soon past. I felt a strange curiosity to know who had been its hapless owner, carrying it safely through twenty or more years of life to lose it here."

Trowbridge viewed the ruins of Richmond, Virginia. Confederates burned all as they retreated from it late in the war.

"All up and down, as far as the eye could reach, the business portion of the city bordering on the river lay in ruins. Beds of cinders, cellars half filled with bricks and rubbish, broken and blackened walls, impassable streets deluged with debris, here a granite front still standing, and there the iron fragments of crushed machinery—such was the scene which extended over thirty entire [square blocks] *and parts of other square* [blocks]*."*

Library of Congress

View of "burnt district," Richmond, VA 1865.

Within months of the war's end, Southern states passed Black Codes. These laws made African Americans slaves once again in all but name. The Black Codes outraged the North and were soon revoked by Congress.

"I remarked to a Mississippi planter, 'Do you not think it was unwise for your Legislature to pass such a code of laws?' 'Yes, it was unwise, at this time,' *he replied, not understanding the scope of my question. 'We showed our hand too soon. We ought to have waited till the* [Union] *troops were withdrawn, and our representatives admitted to Congress; then we could have had everything our own way."*

In Junction, Virginia, a 70-year-old ex-slave was asked about the wages earned by blacks now that they were free. He replied:

"There's nothing said about wages to any of our people in this part of the country. They don't dare ask for them, and their owners will hold them as they used to as long as they can. They are very sharp with us now. If a man of my color dared to say what he thought, it would be all his life was worth!"

Library of Congress

Ruins of Circular Church, Charleston, SC, 1865.

In Memphis, Tennessee, Trowbridge saw a Freedman's school where former slaves were allowed to learn for the first time.

"[Freedman schools] were often held in old buildings and sheds good for little else. There was not a school room in Tennessee furnished with appropriate seats and desks. I found a similar condition of things in all the [Southern] *states. . . .* [Students from ages] *six years to sixty may be seen, side by side, learning to read from the same chart or book. Perhaps a bright little negro boy or girl is teaching a white-haired old man, or bent old woman in spectacles, their letters."*

Hatred of Northerners was widespread. One Georgia planter said:

"If you overheard me [curse] *the Yankees, you'll forgive me, when I tell you how they treated me. [After the war seven Union soldiers] came to my house, put a carbine to my breast, and demanded my watch. 'You may shoot me,' I said, 'but you can't have my watch.' 'Then give us some dinner,' they said. I got dinner for them, and waited on them with my own hands. They paid me for my trouble by stealing seven of my horses."*

But in central Virginia, a Confederate veteran said:

"It is astonishing, when you think of it! Southern men and Northern men ride together in the same trains, and stop at the same hotels, as if we were all one people—as indeed we are: one nation now, he added, as we never were before, and never could have been without the war."

CIVIL WAR K-W-L CHART

In the KWL chart below, write down what you already know about the Civil War in the *K* box, and then write what you want to learn in the *W* box. When you've found the answers to your questions, record your discoveries in the "What I learned" section (*L* box) and new questions next to the "What I still want to learn" section.

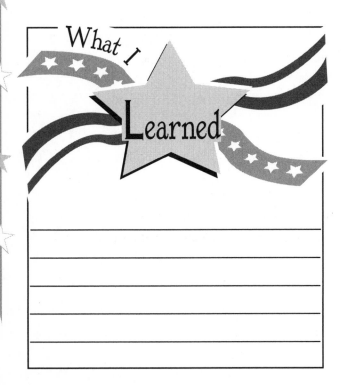

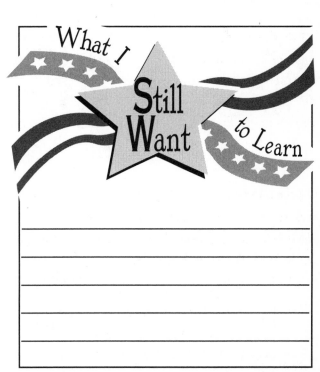

CIVIL WAR MAP

Show what you know about the Union and Confederate states and territories in 1861.

1. Label the states shown on this map. (The shaded states represent territories.)

2. Find the boundary between the Union and Confederate states and territories.

3. Mark the locations of major battles with stars and dates: Bull Run, Gettysburg, Vicksburg, Atlanta, Chattanooga, Antietam, Chancellorsville, Fort Sumter, Mobile Bay, and Appomattox.

4. Color the Union states blue and the Confederate states gray.

CIVIL WAR SPY CODES

Secrecy is vital in wartime. For instance, Union spies knew that the Confederacy was building the submarine C.S.S. *Hunley.* But they did not know when or where it might strike. Part of the reason is that important military messages were written in code. Follow these directions to use the cipher square below and send a secret message to a friend.

1. Before you begin, agree with a partner on a special code sentence. This sentence becomes the key to creating your code. For example, your code sentence might be: *We will rally round the flag.*

2. Choose a message you want to send your partner and write it below the code sentence. For example, your message might be: *Meet me by the oak tree after school.* Make sure you line up your message so each letter is directly under a letter of the code sentence. If your message contains more letters than your code sentence, repeat your code sentence.

WE	WILL	RALLY	ROUND	THE	FLAG	WE	WILL	RALLY		Code Sentence
ME	ETME	BYTHE	OAKTR	EET	ODAY	AF	TERS	CHOOL		Message
II	ABXP	SYESC	FOEGU	XLX	TOAE	WI	PMCD	THZZJ		Encoded Message

3. Take the first letter of your message (M) and find it in the top **row** of the cipher square. Then take the first letter of the code sentence (W) and find it in the first **column**. The place where the row and column meet will be the first letter of your encoded message (I). Continue this process for each of the letter pairs to complete the encoded message.

4. Write the encoded message on a sheet of paper along with the code sentence.

5. Give your partner the message and code sentence, and he or she will work backward to decode the message. For example, start by taking the W in the top row and following the column beneath down to find the I, then tracing across that row to the left to find the M. After successfully completing this process for each of the letter pairs, your partner will get the message!

Message coordinates

Code sentence coordinates

A B C D E F G H I J K L M N O P Q R S T U V W X Y Z
B C D E F G H I J K L M N O P Q R S T U V W X Y Z A
C D E F G H I J K L M N O P Q R S T U V W X Y Z A B
D E F G H I J K L M N O P Q R S T U V W X Y Z A B C
E F G H I J K L M N O P Q R S T U V W X Y Z A B C D
F G H I J K L M N O P Q R S T U V W X Y Z A B C D E
G H I J K L M N O P Q R S T U V W X Y Z A B C D E F
H I J K L M N O P Q R S T U V W X Y Z A B C D E F G
I J K L M N O P Q R S T U V W X Y Z A B C D E F G H
J K L M N O P Q R S T U V W X Y Z A B C D E F G H I
K L M N O P Q R S T U V W X Y Z A B C D E F G H I J
L M N O P Q R S T U V W X Y Z A B C D E F G H I J K
M N O P Q R S T U V W X Y Z A B C D E F G H I J K L
N O P Q R S T U V W X Y Z A B C D E F G H I J K L M
O P Q R S T U V W X Y Z A B C D E F G H I J K L M N
P Q R S T U V W X Y Z A B C D E F G H I J K L M N O
Q R S T U V W X Y Z A B C D E F G H I J K L M N O P
R S T U V W X Y Z A B C D E F G H I J K L M N O P Q
S T U V W X Y Z A B C D E F G H I J K L M N O P Q R
T U V W X Y Z A B C D E F G H I J K L M N O P Q R S
U V W X Y Z A B C D E F G H I J K L M N O P Q R S T
V W X Y Z A B C D E F G H I J K L M N O P Q R S T U
W X Y Z A B C D E F G H I J K L M N O P Q R S T U V
X Y Z A B C D E F G H I J K L M N O P Q R S T U V W
Y Z A B C D E F G H I J K L M N O P Q R S T U V W X
Z A B C D E F G H I J K L M N O P Q R S T U V W X Y

Code Sentence _____

Message _____

Encoded Message _____

Civil War Glossary

Mason Dixon-ary! Use this glossary to understand the meaning of some words and phrases of the Civil War era. Add some other terms to this glossary as you study the Civil War. You may want to incorporate some of these terms as you write your own stories, using the ideas below.

border states
four slave states—Delaware, Kentucky, Maryland, and Missouri—that remained loyal to the Union

carte de visite
a type of photographic calling card popular during the war

Civil War
a war between citizens of the same country

contraband
an escaped slave who sought refuge with Union troops

Dixie
another name for the South (from the song that served as the Confederacy's unofficial anthem)

emancipation
to be freed from slavery

freedman
freed slave

pickets
soldiers who stood guard away from the army to warn of enemy attack

secession
withdrawing from or leaving

states rights
the belief among Southerners that the federal government had limited powers and that states had broad powers

Story Starter Tip!

If you choose to write a story about the experiences of a Confederate or Union soldier during the Civil War, here are some suggestions to get you started:

Dear Brother, My heart is as torn as our nation as I stand on opposite sides of the battlefield from my own flesh and blood . . .

I looked at my men, who were looking at me for their marching orders. I knew some horrible facts I could not share with them, lest their spirits fall. I knew the position and strength of our opponents, and I knew how low our supplies were running. I called them to attention and said, ". . .

It was the darkest hour of the night when I made my escape. Just as I had been told, someone was waiting for me . . .

My friend was lying in the ditch bleeding, but still alive. "Go ahead," he told me. But I could not . . .

I sat in the parlor at Appomattox, waiting for Grant. I knew he had received my letter. Now we were about to come face to face. I sat straight in my full-dress uniform, ready to surrender my sword.

CIVIL WAR JOURNAL

_____

_____

_____

_____

_____

_____

_____

_____

_____

_____

_____

_____

_____

_____

_____

_____

_____

_____

_____

_____

_____

_____

_____

_____

_____

_____

_____

_____

_____

CIVIL WAR MAP ANSWER KEY

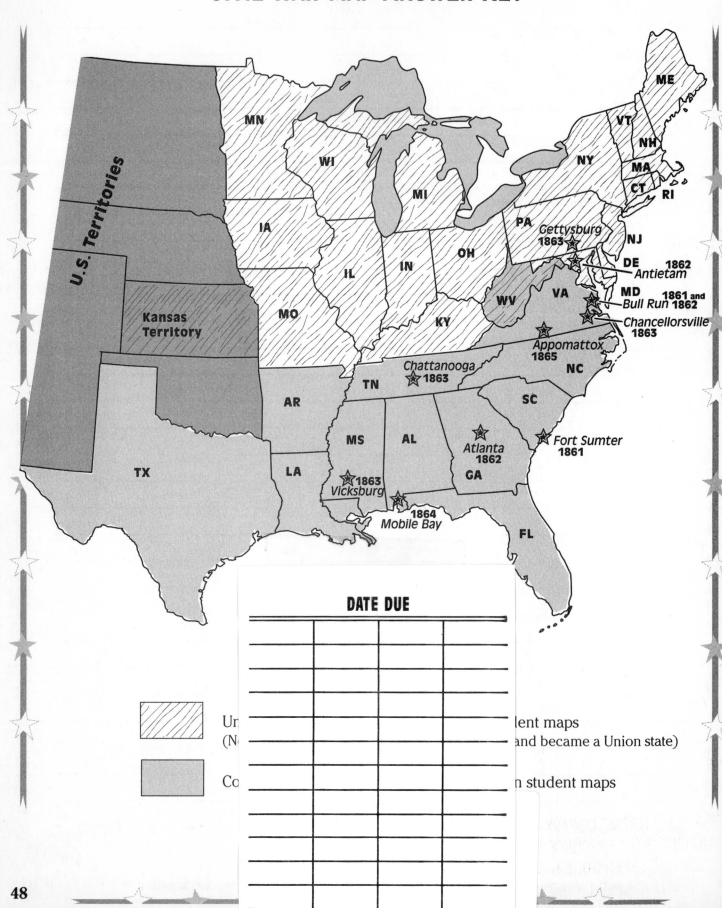

ME

VT

NH

NY

MA

CT

RI

MN

WI

MI

PA

Gettysburg 1863

NJ

IA

OH

DE 1862

Antietam

IL

IN

WV

VA

MD 1861 and

Bull Run 1862

U.S. Territories

MO

KY

Chancellorsville 1863

Kansas Territory

Appomattox 1865

Chattanooga 1863

NC

TN

SC

AR

MS

AL

Atlanta 1862

Fort Sumter 1861

TX

LA

GA

1863
Vicksburg

1864
Mobile Bay

FL

DATE DUE

Un_____lent maps
(N_____and became a Union state)

Co_____n student maps